Vertical development in the workplace

PETER BLUCKERT

Published by Peter Bluckert.

www.peterbluckert.com

Copyright © Peter Bluckert 2019

First Published 2019.

ISBN 978-1-9161300-2-9

Typeset and illustrated by Adam Thorp

Section 1

Section 2

Section 1

Chapter 1.
The rationale for vertical development

Introduction

Much of the literature on the 'what' and the 'why' of vertical development is set within the organisational context, focusing on the developmental needs of leaders in response to the VUCA world. The argument goes like this: due to the rapid pace of change, volatility and uncertainty (V&U), complexity and ambiguity (C&A), leaders are increasingly in over their heads, requiring them to grow bigger minds and develop a higher capacity to deal with the ever more challenging 'wicked' problems of our time. Those working closely with leaders as trusted advisors would probably agree with this, aware that many of their clients are struggling, and pointing to the high levels of executive stress as compelling evidence.

And anyone who works in senior roles in business, public service, political or not-for-profit organisations will recognise this proposition. In fact, anyone who works in any sort of organisation will probably recognise it – as well as millions more who have never worked in one but nonetheless experience life as more complicated and complex. So, we can say that this is an issue for organisational leaders for sure, and this is also an issue for everyone else because previous ways of making sense of things, and ways of reacting, don't always seem to work anymore. The outer game of work and life has changed, and many people are struggling to adapt to it.

This short book is part of the Expand the Possible series, written specifically for organisational leaders, emerging leaders, their professional helpers, and indeed anyone working in the organisational context. For those readers interested in the wider application of vertical growth and development in all spheres of life, I point you to my longer book – 'Expand the Possible: The Gestalt Approach to Vertical Growth and Development'.

Note: If you're not already familiar with adult development theory, you may want to begin with the first short book in this Expand the Possible series, 'A Comprehensive Guide to Vertical Growth and Development' – an introduction to the field – see www.courageandspark.com

Embarkation point

When you read about vertical development, or deeper self-exploration processes of any kind, you might find yourself wondering if the authors are preparing you for an international expedition – an outer-world journey, into new and undiscovered territory. Yet, this is a quite different expedition because essentially, it's an inner journey – a developmental journey.

Similar to the outer journeys of life, there are optional and non-optional elements.

The non-optional part is that life experiences will take you there whether you want to go or not. They already have. The optional element is a question of decision and requires a combination of commitment, and proactivity, and effective support.

The agenda for vertical development in the workplace:

1. To assist organisational leaders manage complexity and change.

2. To fast-track high-potential talent, and assist them to develop the capacities they'll need in senior leadership roles.

3. To help current and future leaders consolidate at their current vertical stage of development.

4. To help current and future leaders become more balanced across all the lines of personal development: physical; cognitive; emotional; ego maturity; behavioural; impact and connection; and ethical.

5. To maximize the power of transformative development to facilitate self-actualisation and fulfil personal and collective potential.

6. To minimise the risk that people run out of competence due to not paying sufficient attention to their growth and development.

7. To help leaders connect more strongly with colleagues, transform working relationships, and in turn, the larger leadership culture.

Current and future leaders need all the support and help they can get to meet the demands of their roles and those they will move into, so that there is less likelihood of a mismatch between role and capacity. Helping build new capacities to deal with the ever more challenging and demanding leadership context is a significant part of the remit for vertical development in the workplace.

Chapter 2.
An introduction to vertical development

Horizontal learning and vertical development

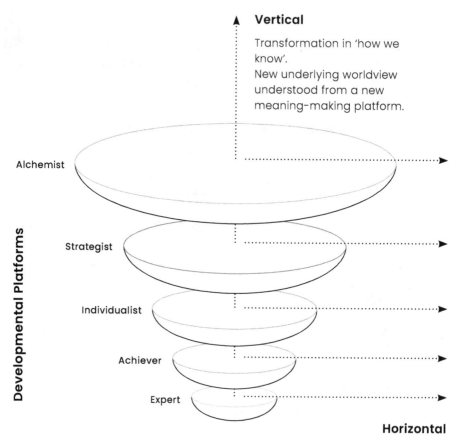

Vertical

Transformation in 'how we know'.
New underlying worldview understood from a new meaning-making platform.

Alchemist

Strategist

Individualist

Achiever

Expert

Developmental Platforms

Horizontal

Expansion in 'what we know' (new skills, new information, new knowledge) but understood from the same meaning-making platform.

Recent interest in horizontal and vertical development has brought to people's attention that most leadership development processes, and learning in general, has been based on the premise that if we equip people with knowledge, new skills, abilities and behaviours, then those will later translate into improved competency and performance. This paradigm is a technical one where problems can be broken down, analysed and fixed so long as we have acquired the necessary technical knowledge to deal with them.

An analogy frequently used to describe horizontal development is the act of pouring water into a glass. As more knowledge, skills and competencies are acquired, the glass fills up. When deficits are identified, the answer is to find new or better ones to put into the glass. People who search for new tools, techniques and models are effectively on the same mission – to fill their glass. From this perspective, excellence in management and leadership, or for that matter, any form of practice, is achieved by filling the glass with the best possible content available.

How vertical compliments horizontal

Horizontal development =

adding more knowledge, skills and competencies. (Filling the glass with more content)

Vertical approaches =

grows the internal capacities to operate in more complex, systemic, strategic and interdependent ways.

Expands an individual's ability to handle complexity and 'sense make' in ambiguous and uncertain situations. (Increases the glass size or leader's worldview)

Given that most education systems and professional and leadership development programmes are based on the horizontal paradigm, it's hardly surprising that many people only understand learning and development from this point of view. And it would be absurd to dismiss the importance of knowledge acquisition and proper training to perform proficiently. Business managers need to understand profit and loss accounts, company procedures and good HR practice. Leaders need to understand how to turn around the financial performance of their organisations and enable them to flourish. Core skills, informational content and technical expertise are all required in any professional discipline. Without it people would flounder or worse still, make disastrous mistakes. So, it goes without saying that horizontal learning is necessary and is important at each and every stage of adult development. It expands the breadth of one's information, knowledge, and skills.

However, the image of the two glasses makes the powerful point that whilst traditional, horizontal learning fills the glass, vertical development increases the size of the glass. We literally become more spacious, bigger people.

Vertical development

'Who looks outside, dreams,
Who looks inside, awakens' – Jung

Vertical development is the process of learning to see the world through new eyes and changing the interpretations and meanings we ascribe to life experience. It largely requires an inside-out approach to learning, quite different in nature to the outside-in horizontal method. Vertical development is based on reflection, awareness-raising and personal insight, and requires deeper self-examination and personal work. In turn, this can lead to changes in perspective and an increased capacity to see, understand, empathise, and be in stronger contact with ourselves, others, and the world.

It's important to recognise that horizontal and vertical development paths are not an either-or. On the contrary, they work together. Skill and knowledge from horizontal development often require reflective practice and feedback which can then lead to increased awareness. Combining this with a willingness to be changed by awareness and experience, critical to vertical development, can transform how we come to know ourselves and influence our world.

When individuals evolve to a later stage of adult development it is the result of both horizontal learning and vertical development – the acquisition of knowledge, skills and behaviours together with psychological, emotional and spiritual development. This is a virtuous circle in that inner change alters outer behaviours. For example, as a person matures, deals with more of their unresolved and unfinished situations, we generally see less defensiveness and volatility, the need to control and be right, or to offer uninvited opinions and advice.

Learning to let go

In contrast to horizontal learning, vertical development is as much about unlearning as learning. Indeed, one of its key features, and an important reason why it's so difficult, is that it so often involves letting go of something. And in turn that produces a felt sense that we're at risk – we're going to lose someone or something.

Loss, and the fear of it, combined with the vulnerability that's associated with it, is part of the vertical development terrain. It can be the letting go of certainty, and a re-assessment of strongly held beliefs and assumptions. Or the loss of previous ways of seeing the world. But it's not so much that these were wrong; rather, we come to see that they were incomplete.

It can be letting go of the identity we've formed around something we've created. Or the letting go of the story we re-tell about ourselves which we've come to realise is no longer accurate, or even true. It can be letting go of our need to look good, to over-control or be right.

Perhaps the most powerful and difficult thing many of us need to let go is our habit of living with excessive fear, self-doubt and an over-sized inner critic. And to replace that with a kinder, more gentle and compassionate relationship with ourselves.

None of this is easy but by letting go, our perspective evolves and we change. And we often find that we travel lighter into our futures.

The process of vertical development involves inner change, psychological breakthroughs and emotional contact, and is not always visible to the untrained eye. Sometimes it's only months or years later that people notice and say – there's something different about you now.

Cognitive understanding of vertical development can be a useful starting point and may create a shift of consciousness. However, on its own, it's unlikely to be enough. The journey of vertical development is primarily an experiential one. So, just as reading about emotional intelligence doesn't necessarily lead to an improvement in EQ, reading about developmental and complexity theory doesn't transition a person to the next stage nor fundamentally change their developmental centre of gravity.

To grow a more conscious mind often begins with freeing the mind. Many of us know that we are still captured by a combination of the external circumstances of our lives and historical unfinished experiences that continue to impact in present time. We know this because we regularly find ourselves snagged or re-stimulated.

If we are still locked into the technical worldview where every problem and dilemma can be broken down, analysed and fixed in the same way as engineering issues can be resolved, then we may run the risk of wasting a great deal of our energy and time going around and around the same spirals. Many of life's more complex and challenging problems are of a different nature and require a very different approach to them – adaptive change. A change in ourselves. That's not to say there aren't times when we do need to alter some of those material circumstances of our life to become freed up again. What we may miss, however, is that these exterior-focused changes don't always transform things. In these circumstances, we need to be looking elsewhere and recognise that the breakthrough we're looking for has to be an interior change.

A summary of key vertical development propositions

'Everything can be seen directly except… the eye through which we see' E.F. Schumacher, The Guide for the Perplexed. 1977.

- Horizontal learning at one's current stage is as important as vertical development towards the next. In fact, the optimal developmental strategy is a combination of both horizontal learning and vertical development.

- Our worldview and our filters, which includes our core beliefs, assumptions, attitudes and value judgements, acts as our frame of reference for interpreting the meaning of our experience. Some researchers believe that a person's frame of reference determines what they pay attention to and consider important, filtering everything else out.

- Most people have some awareness of their worldview but their filters are the eyes through which they see. This sets the purpose of vertical development which is to enable us to understand more about those filters which fundamentally shape how we make sense of the world. We may then choose to hold onto, let go or change them.

- The way in which we see more, and understand our filters, has been described by Kegan and Lahey as the Subject-Object shift. What was formerly in the unknown space (where we are subject to it) moves into the known space (where we can more objectively perceive it). Something comes out of the dark into the light and can be reflected upon.

- But this is more than reflecting on something new or a part of ourselves that has been previously repressed, disowned or buried. In Kegan's (1994) language, 'we have Object, we are Subject'. And once we have something, we are responsible, we have choices and decisions to make, we can act.

- The changing Subject-Object relationship defines developmental growth and propels stage change.

- Using the Kegan language, each of the stage changes – from socialised to self-authored to self-transforming – amounts to a fundamental restructuring of mind.

- With each fundamental shift that happens, the individual is more capable of dealing with complex environments and challenges. Research with organisational leaders suggests this significantly improves their effectiveness.

- When leaders struggle, or ultimately fail in their roles, the typical interpretation is the Peter Principle: that they've run out of capability. It's a competency issue. A vertical perspective would be that they've reached the limit of their development, not necessarily their capability. There is a mismatch between their level of development, and consciousness, and the complexities they're facing into.

- Complexity includes both outer dynamics such as the rapidly accelerating pace of change; and the inner dynamics of our personal lives.

- Kegan and Lahey describe it as: "When we experience the world as 'too complex', we're not just experiencing the complexity of the world. We are experiencing a mismatch between the world's complexity and our own at this moment. There are only two logical ways to mend this mismatch – reduce the world's complexity or increase your own".

- Given the world's complexity isn't going to slow down, it's more likely to accelerate, we really only have one choice.

Vertical development applied to organisational leadership

- An individual's stage of development significantly affects how they understand their role, function and value in work and wider life, how they interact with others, and how they deal with adversity and complex issues. Indeed, it predicts how one even defines problems in the first place; for example, as a technical issue that has a specific solution if only we can find it, or as an adaptive challenge where the change is not in the outer game but in the inner game – within yourself.

  - A number of research studies show that a very high proportion of managers and leaders (75-80%, depending on the study) are at the conventional stage of development – in the language of Action Logics, diplomat, expert, and achiever stages of adult development.

- In Western cultures, the achiever stage is the pinnacle of conventional adult development.

- In many ways, this is good news. To run any enterprise, you need experts and highly competent, results-focused, driven, achievement-oriented people. How else do you solve problems, get things done and achieve results?

- For many, the main currency at these stages is knowledge, information (data) and expertise. At expert and achiever, people tend to preference four things – knowing more, doing more, achieving more, and advancement. At the transition of expert/achiever, where a high percentage of managers and leaders profile, being busy, often overbusy, becomes a key feature of their lives. Action, at pace, provides stimulation, excitement, challenge and huge satisfaction – especially when it's going well, their career progression timetable is on schedule, and the financial rewards are keeping up with expectation.

- Readers at these stages may recognise themselves in this description but rightly argue that it is partial and oversimplified. It should also be noted that, as people mature in these stages, they can also become highly reflective, curious, sensitive, interpersonally skilled, strategically aware, excellent leaders.

- For those people who transition to individualist, this picture starts to look different. What used to give them a buzz doesn't quite do it anymore. They can still perform the 'outer game of business' but it isn't everything anymore. New questions and concerns are emerging in their 'inner game'. Uncomfortable times can lie ahead as colleagues begin to pick up on their disquiet and question their commitment to the common purpose and collective core assumptions that we need all hands to the pumps and succeeding is everything. This can be tempered by what they also recognise as some valuable new perspectives, intelligent questions and useful critiquing. They may see this as thinking outside the box.

- Over-extended leaders caught up in the frenetic maelstrom don't always see the cost of the excessive hours and pressures on their energy, health, well-being and relationships. Many are living with high levels of exhaustion, stress, anxiety and pain. They don't know how to switch off. So, their periods of calm become increasingly rare. And for some, this only surfaces when they're already in an advanced stage of burnout or when their core relationships are in crisis. Perhaps, they've felt 'in over their heads' for some time but how do you say that to anyone when you don't even want to admit it to yourself.

- The accelerating pace of change and complexity is putting an evolutionary demand on leaders that we keep pace, or better still, more than match it by increasing our complexity of mind. This won't be achieved through more and more horizontal learning, even if it's from the very best academic institutes. Leaders also need to grow and develop vertically and recognise that inner, adaptive change will often be more important than outer, technical solutions.

- Laloux (2014) in his book 'Reinventing Organisations' was one of the first to apply stage development to organisations but is careful to stress that speaking of organisations as red, orange, green or teal, refers to their structures, practices, policies and cultures; not the stage development of their people nor the defining nature of social interaction. Clearly, in any sizeable organisation there will be a range of individual stages represented as the studies have shown. The highest proportion in most organisations will be in the conventional tier (diplomat, expert and achiever), with a far smaller number in preconventional (opportunist), and postconventional (individualist, strategist and alchemist).

- Research findings suggest that later stage, postconventional leaders – strategist and beyond - are more successful at leading organisational transformations. They have a greater capacity to deal with complexity, a higher psychological understanding of people, heightened emotional intelligence and a deeper appreciation of cultural dynamics. They are more welcoming of diverse ideas and perspectives, and can see more patterns and inter-connections. They not only see the dots but also can join them up. And this in turn can lead to more creative solutions.

- However, the studies indicate that there are only around 8% of leaders at these stages of evolutionary growth at present and many executive teams don't possess any. This is sometimes mitigated by the presence of a later stage consultant or coach who has the ear of the CEO and the team.

- In an ever more challenging world this has brought many developmentalists to a similar conclusion. That the most significant priority in the leadership development space today is to find ways of accelerating the journey from the achiever to strategist stage of development. In his paper, Organisational Transformation requires the presence of leaders who are Strategists and Alchemists, Rooke (1997), states; 'my proposition is that only managers at the postconventional stages, Individualist and later, can steer transformational culture change. Managers at earlier stages would either not see the need or seeing it, would not have the inclusive frame-making ability to realise it. Even at the Individualist stage, the differentiated ability in transformational meaning-making and action is limited. Only at the Strategist stage does this capacity emerge with any possibility of consistency.'

- When we consider the implications of this proposition beyond the realm of business leadership and apply it to the political, social, economic and ecological challenges facing the world, it's full significance becomes ever more obvious.

Chapter 3.
Optimal workplace conditions for vertical development

Table 3.1.
Optimal workplace conditions for vertical development

Working in coaching cultures and intentionally developmental organisations.

Stretch experiences, assignments and roles.

Developmental conversations with line managers and internal HR business partners and coaches.

Time with late stage mentors.

Membership of action learning sets, peer groups, networks and communities of practice.

Working in coaching cultures and intentionally developmental organisations

Working in a growth culture and having regular access to coaching-style leaders is a key factor in accelerated vertical development. Whilst some first-line managers and senior leaders don't feel comfortable with taking a coaching approach, most organisations possess a number of 'naturals'. These coaching-style leaders understand their first concern needs to be their own performance, and improving it by every means possible. But they also look to the growth and development of all those working for and around them. Some even measure their own progress by the growth of others. When you speak to these people, they often say that this is the most enjoyable part of their jobs.

They tend to share a number of common beliefs and practices:

- They believe that learning is important and ongoing.

- They encourage their people to reflect on their work performance, take responsibility for their own development and be open to feedback.

- They are aware that opportunities exist every day to help people learn and improve if the coachable moments are spotted and well used.

- They value the importance of quality conversations and commit time to having them.

- They create an expectation that coaching conversations occur routinely as 'the way we do things around here'.

- They understand the critical importance of providing effective and sufficient support.

Employees committed to their own growth agendas are drawn to working with these kinds of leaders because they know they will develop more quickly. This makes coaching-style leaders a great asset to their immediate team members but also to their organisations as they are key enablers of the next-generation leadership pipeline.

These coaching-style leaders also value the learning they derive from the conversations. They appreciate that in a genuine coaching conversation, feedback is a two-way street, not simply a top-down process. The leader potentially gains as much as they give and for this reason, becoming a coaching-style leader, can of itself be a significant vertical development accelerator.

And when leaders develop vertically, their perspective on what leadership is about and what it really takes to transform their organisations evolves to a more sophisticated level. The technical worldview where everything is a problem to be solved and we just need to use the correct tools and processes, begins to dissolve. A new appreciation around adaptive change begins to replace it and, as a consequence of that, they arrive at a new appreciation that change really must start with them, however difficult that is. This can lead to a more empowering leadership style and an intention to build a more developmental culture. In turn, they become clearer that their own role needs to change. They recognise the need to involve people more, seek out feedback, loosen control and grapple with multiple perspectives. Managing change begins to look like a flawed concept; transformational leadership fits better with the newly emerging mindset.

A commitment to higher levels of emotional intelligence and accelerated vertical development, both at the senior leadership level and throughout the organisation, goes hand in hand with this. If, at moments of truth, leaders fail to let go of sufficient control to enable innovation and support risk-taking, then they are inevitably perceived as the limiters rather than facilitators of growth. It's in these moments when power is seized back, even when there are other justifications, that trust is compromised and precious ground lost.

Raising the bar on culture and setting a vertical development agenda for an organisation therefore carries with it significant implications for individual and team development. The inter-connection between the outer game of business performance and the inner process of psychological and emotional development becomes obvious to those who make the journey. Without vertical development at senior leadership levels, the ceiling remains in place.

Organisational transformation mirrors a multitude of personal transformations

On the other hand, when there is the presence of later stage development leaders, and they set out to create more progressive organisational cultures, those contexts can pull people up and they can achieve outcomes they would not have thought possible. These more developmentally oriented cultures become very special places to work in because there is a sense that everyone is growing and succeeding together. These can be the circumstances where genuine organisational transformation mirrors a multitude of personal transformations.

For some people, it will only be these kinds of organisations, with a more conscious leadership, that will appeal to them. They will search out these beacon organisations but may still exit them if they don't find a culture that matches and keeps pace with their own desires to grow and develop.

Stretch experiences, assignments and roles

If you have been promoted or taken on stretch roles, projects and assignments you'll probably look back and recognise the huge developmental value they afforded you. Perhaps you didn't always think you'd be able to step up to what was required, and maybe you wondered why you were being given such an opportunity. You may have struggled for longer than you would have liked – searching for some solid ground under your feet.

If your promotion was to a senior team, perhaps it took you longer than you expected to feel like a genuinely equal member of your new team. You may have suffered the classic imposter syndrome – feeling like you really didn't belong. But hopefully you came through, and in the process, grew. These stretch experiences may have set a pattern of regularly looking for the next challenging assignment. In a sense, you've developed the habit of doing two jobs – your current one whilst on the look-out for the next one.

Many organisations, and especially those with developmental and fast-paced cultures, rapidly rotate their high potential talent and the typical life cycle of 'catapult' roles and stretch assignments has come down to as little as 9-18 months. These 'heat experiences' as Petrie (2015) calls them, tend to follow a similar pattern:

- At first, you feel in over your head but scramble to work out how to stay afloat.

- You then start to get the hang of it and performance and results improve.

- And then you experience some mastery, begin to get bored and restless, and start looking around for more heat.

Living and working in a different culture

Or if you've lived and worked in another country, with a very different culture, you may see this as one of your golden periods. Your need to learn, and the rate at which you learned, was atypical of the previous chapter of your life. Your assumptions didn't quite fit your new circumstances. Their 'realities' were similar to yours; but also, different. They didn't always see the world in the way you did. So, it forced you to reflect and re-evaluate. You were less able to take things for granted.

One of the most significant vertical development catalysts can be the change from being in an individual contributor role to team leadership. The reason for this is that it requires a shift from an 'I' self-centric perspective to a 'we' group-centric perspective. Team leadership can be a growing-up experience where the responsibility for other people's lives and well-being becomes an accelerator of ego maturity. It creates a new need - the appreciation of other people's contributions and the larger context of care – not just for results but for them as people. It also calls on you to expand your repertoire of skills and behaviours, not least in the emotional intelligence space.

What these experiences have in common is that they disturb your equilibrium and take you out of your comfort zone. Your beliefs about people and life, many of which will have been invisible to you because they are the lens you see life through, are thrown into a melting-pot. You have to re-assess, let go of something, and take something new on-board. It can be a confusing experience and one where you feel an increased sense of vulnerability. Your ways of thinking and making sense of the world are challenged. What's got you to this stage doesn't quite seem to be enough anymore in these new circumstances. Perhaps even your sense of who you are, your identity, is called into question.

These kinds of growth experiences stretch your capability (not necessarily competence), and this can be precisely what's needed to accelerate vertical development. However, and this is an important consideration, they don't facilitate growth and development if you are simply overloaded, over-stressed and floored by the new demands. In these circumstances people can lose direction and self-confidence. As such, the level of challenge within these stretch opportunities needs to be matched by sufficient support. When that's not available, you have to rely too much on yourself for self-support. This can be growthful in the longer term, but in the short term can lead to performance issues. It may also establish, or reinforce, a psychological pattern of over-independence and over self-reliance.

Developmental conversations with line managers and internal HR business partners and coaches

The places people look for that support in the work environment are their line managers, HR business partners, and friends. Line manager support, and wisdom, in setting people up to succeed is critical to achieving desired outcomes when individuals are given developmental challenges and stretch roles. Indeed, the quality of relationship with a line manager, and the quality of the feedback provided by them, is a significant factor in personal well-being and on-the-job vertical development.

Line manager support is often perceived as more important in the earlier phases of an individuals' leadership career, when some of the challenges of team leadership and stretch roles are still relatively new and unfamiliar. This can become less important when you acquire greater competency in task and people management.

Seasoned leaders use their trusted internal HR business partners and external coaches more readily as confidantes for personal and developmental issues, reserving their conversations with their bosses for strategic content and career development.

How to hold productive, positive developmental conversations with direct reports remains one of the most common developmental needs for many line managers and senior leaders. HR business partners are often asked to advise on this. These leaders recognise their important role in the ongoing development of their team members but may lack the confidence and competence to coach on anything other than task-related content. At some stage of their careers leaders tend to be introduced to coaching models such as GROW and be offered a day or two of coaching skills training. However, that rarely seems enough to equip them to go beyond a goal-focused coaching conversation. Being asked to coach people on their developmental-edge seems like a step too far. It also raises the question about whether this is really a part of their role anyway, given the power imbalance.

In light of this, internal developmental coaching is often referred on to more highly trained business partners or learning and development specialists. In some companies, there are people operating as internal executive coaches usually located in the Talent and Leadership functions. Their role is to support leaders in their developmental journeys and support them with elevated sense-making and perspective-taking. Some of these internal coaches have taken specialist coach training in vertical coaching and are able to offer this to their organisational leaders.

Having this resource within an organisation can play a significant part in accelerating vertical development amongst the leadership population. Leaders have access to more advanced, skilled coaching to explore their current challenges, reflect on career progression issues and face into potential career derailment issues. If they are preparing to attend a leadership programme, or returning from one, they can use this coaching to fine-tune what they hope to gain, and later process what they've learnt from it. This developmental coaching can help consolidate and integrate the benefits of the structured learning experience.

Membership of peer groups, action learning sets, networks and communities of practice

The number of executive networking groups, peer coaching groups and action learning sets has grown in recent years as people have discovered the benefits of having a regular place, with a consistent group membership, to air their concerns, get help with their challenges and receive support for their personal growth.

Harthill in their Leadership Development Framework (LDF) profile report make the explicit point that at later stage adult development it's important to "explore with others, of like minds, who have experienced the trials of self-discovery. Seek members of your community of practice who wish to work together to mentor one another's continuing development."

These sorts of ongoing groups often begin their life as groups of individuals attending a leadership programme. The power of the bonding experience can be something people don't want to lose so they make a commitment to some form of networking or peer group.

Action learning has spread as an idea rather than as a specific method, as devised by Revans in the 1960's, and there are now wide variations in its practice. Most current practice focuses on 'own job' projects and personal development, rather than on organisational problems which was Revans' original vision. The value of these groups derives from having a safe, trusted space to share problems and receive quality attention, peer coaching and outside perspective. It's not unusual for people to feel that they are the only one with the problem they struggle with. When they take the risk of sharing it they are often pleasantly surprised, and re-assured that they aren't the only one.

Over time, membership of these kinds of peer groups can have significant impact on how people feel about opening up, being more transparent and risking their vulnerability. A commonly held view of corporate life, that it's not wise to reveal 'weakness' – on the contrary, it's downright stupid to do so – gets whittled down to size. In some cases, it gets transformed through the regular experience of taking risks and gaining huge benefits from it. The possibilities of intimate connection with colleagues at work magnify. What was once a deeply held assumption, a personal truth about the way corporates are, begins to change.

Time with later stage mentors

As Petrie (2015) notes:

"A powerful developmental experience is spending time with a mentor who is operating from a later stage of development. If you have ever had this experience, you can't help but notice that these mentors ask different questions than you and that their perspectives don't mesh with the way you see the world... If your readiness is right, they can also help you start to create new maps of reality that are more suited to where your career and life might be headed. The experience of partnering with late-stage thinkers can be both discomforting and enlightening ... and can act as a powerful pull to later stages".

Whilst this form of vertical development may at first sight seem more appropriate for high-potentials and younger emerging leaders, it can be just as helpful to more experienced managers and leaders. Indeed, the isolating nature of senior leadership means that many executives are short of the meaning-making conversations they need to negotiate complexity. But the issue is not simply about the reducing number of people they can talk to, because most people don't need 5 or 10 or 20. What they value is a small number of people who they can trust to provide perspective when their own eludes them.

These people will probably be at the same developmental stage, or more likely, one beyond their own. This enables the mentor to see them and 'get' them. The subtleties and nuances are understood in ways that validate and affirm.

Elevated sense-making is a thinking and feeling process.

The best relationships of this kind create a holding space where you can not only think your way through challenges and dilemmas but also feel safe enough to experience your confusion, self-doubt and fear. Much of the vertical development literature privileges thinking using such terms as growing a bigger mind. This can give the false impression that vertical development is essentially a cognitive, intellectual process. In practice, cognitive development is necessary but often insufficient. Memorable conversations occur when a safe environment and strong trust enables people to feel what they feel as well as think what they think.

Indeed, it's often when people more deeply connect with what they feel about an experience, that they make significant breakthroughs. If the conversation stays too 'heady' there can be a sense that the important learning has remained out of range. This is the true meaning of emotional intelligence – that our emotions contain intelligence if we risk bringing them into play. At the same time, this requires the mentor to also be sufficiently comfortable with their own emotions, and the expression of emotions in their mentee.

So, when looking for a late stage mentor, it's important to discover whether they do have the capacity to ask those different kinds of questions and bring new perspectives. And it's equally important that you will be able to have those conversations you can't find anywhere else. Conversations that take you to new frontiers because that's where the growth will take place.

Section 2

Chapter 4.
The organisational context as an enabler (and disabler) of vertical development

It's important to recognise that context and environment shapes and creates us, just as we shape and co-create it. This becomes more evident to people when they begin to appreciate that if they change their way of reacting in a relationship, the wider dynamic inevitably shifts. It simply can't stay the same.

Almost all depth psychologies work from the premise that we can only ever begin to understand people when we also take the time and trouble to understand their contexts and their worlds. It's the combination of intra-personal (inner) and contextual (outer) factors that forms the person, and it's precisely the same two factors that determine the rate of an individual's vertical development.

Those people who have worked for different organisations, or different parts of the same organisation, understand the significance of organisational context and culture to their growth possibilities. And, the important part that leaders and managers play in this. Culture opens things up, and closes things off.

Laloux (2014), was one of the first writers to apply vertical development theory to organisations in terms of their structures, practices, policies and cultures. Note that he wasn't referring to the stage development of their people nor the defining nature of social interaction. His analysis was not at the intra-personal or inter-personal level. He was interested to discover whether the structures, practices and policies might reveal a centre of gravity that pervades the 'main' organisational culture.

Using the Spiral Dynamics adult development framework with its colour referencing system, he identified the different characteristics of red, amber, orange, green and teal organisational cultures.

In summary:

Red organisations constantly use command authority and power to keep people in line. Fear is the glue of the organisation. Highly reactive and short-term focus. A good decision is the one that gets me what I want.

Amber organisations exhibit top-down, hierarchical control through highly formal roles. Stability is kept through rigorous processes. Future is repetition of the past.

Orange organisations aim to beat competition, achieve profit and growth. Innovation is the key to staying ahead. Management by objectives (command and control of what; freedom on the how). Orange organisations are achievement focused, where rationality, effectiveness and success are the yardsticks by which decisions are made.

Green organisations focus more on culture and empowerment to achieve high employee engagement and motivation. Belonging, engagement and harmony become increasingly important.

Teal organisations reflect a different relationship with power and authority and focus more on trust, purpose, fulfilment of potential, and community/societal impact."

He concluded that whilst there are likely to be pockets of different ways of operating which reflect a different stage of consciousness, typically as a direct result of later stage leadership and where there is scope for autonomy, in the main, the culture will be a reflection of the developmental stage of its senior leadership.

In other words, without necessarily being conscious of it, the organisational structures, practices, policies and cultures emerge from the worldview of the senior leadership, with all that is positive about that, and with all the limitations that go with any worldview.

As leaders develop vertically, their perspective on what it really takes to transform their organisations evolves to a more sophisticated level. They understand the role of leadership differently and they see their people differently. The conventional technical mindset which says everything can be predicted and problems broken down and solved in a rational fashion begins to look like a partial rather than absolute truth. A new appreciation emerges that there are some challenges which simply can't be solved in this way. They require a qualitatively different approach – one that's based on the notion of adaptive change. They come to a true appreciation that change really must start, and continue, with them.

This is a pivotal change which many senior leaderships teams have yet to arrive at but if they do, it typically leads to more empowered leadership styles, a coaching culture ethos, an embracing of difference and a deeper respect for multiple perspectives on what needs to be done and how. It becomes evident that a number of new capacities will be required both at the most senior levels of the organisation and cascading throughout it. These include new competencies which can be learnt through skills training programmes but also require the more conscious leadership behaviours and larger perspectives which emerge from vertical growth and development.

When there is the presence of later stage development leaders, and they set out to create more progressive organizational cultures, these contexts can pull people up and they can achieve outcomes previously not thought possible. These more developmentally oriented cultures become very special places to work because there is a sense that everyone is growing and succeeding together. These can be the circumstances where genuine organisational transformation mirrors a multitude of personal transformations.

For some people, it will only be these kinds of organisations, with this more conscious leadership, that will appeal to them. They will search out these beacon organisations but may still exit them if they don't find a culture that matches and keeps pace with their own desires to grow and develop.

Chapter 5.
Mapping the developmental journey and stage profiling

Mapping the developmental journey

Organisations that embark on the vertical development journey can find it helpful to present their leaders with maps, in the form of one or more of the adult development frameworks that show what it might mean to transform to a new vertical stage. This can be the way into a conversation that provides a deeper insight into what vertical development really looks and feels like - and what it is that actually grows and changes. This mapping conversation can demystify how transformational change typically unfolds over time: involving periods on a plateau; breakthroughs, shifts and fall-backs; transitions between stages; and periods of consolidation and integration at the new stage. It can be re-assuring to hear that feeling stuck and regressing from time to time are standard experiences in the developmental journey. It's just normal.

In my own leadership consultancy work with organisations I offer individual and group-based conversations to set out the purpose of developmental mapping which I see as:

- Assisting managers and leaders to pursue their personal growth and development with greater clarity, focus and perspective.

- Helping them to understand the importance of consolidating and integrating at their current vertical stage, in contrast to rushing on to the next.

- Showing how a vertical development journey can unfold and what their next stage of development might look and feel like.

- Explaining how individual coaching, group-based workshops, and structured leadership development programmes can support them in their journey.

- Helping them to consider the best developmental routes for them to take, and whether this is the right time.

- Elevating the developmental conversations they have with those they manage and lead.

In short, the 'mapping conversation' can help people to better understand who they have been up until now, and paint some pictures of what next – or who next.

Finally, one of the important benefits of having a mapping conversation from the internal coach's perspective, is that it provides an opportunity to assess developmental motivation and understand the individual's inner driving forces for growth. And even if the time is not right now, the conversation is likely to seed a curiosity and accelerate the pace of future development.

'When looking at a long span of human history, it is usually possible to identify signs of both social evolution and devolution. But it is always hard to put the present into a bigger framework that lets us know where we are and where we are headed. And this is as true for individuals as it is for human society. This is the reason we need maps of the territory we pass through as we awaken and begin to unfold. Without such maps, it is almost inevitable that we limit the possibilities of human transformation … we settle for far too little'

Benner (2012).

Stage profiling - helping people understand their current developmental stage and consolidating

It's important to stress that people have a range of reactions to vertical stage theory. Some of the definitions leave a lot to be desired in terms of clean language and definitions such as Expert and Achiever can rankle with some people who see them as labels. And it's not uncommon for people to experience these terms as judgemental and hierarchical. I say this because not every manager and leader is going to react positively and favourably to the invitation to understand their current developmental stage. Some will be drawn to stage assessment profiles and others will be resistant. So, if that's the case, it's important to respect the person's viewpoint and leave well alone.

It's also important to recognise that some achievement-oriented managers and leaders will expect to profile at a later stage than their report indicates, and consequently may be disappointed and de-motivated by the process. If they are used to excelling at everything, they may translate the stages to mean: A, B, C and D. Having always strived to be an A and maybe achieved it most of the time, anything that doesn't say A can come as a shock to the system. This reinforces the importance of properly explaining the developmental stages and journey prior to any discussion about whether to take an assessment profile.

It's equally important to stress that stage definitions are at best approximations, not 'reality', and that a person is never simply at one stage. We all fluctuate around a particular stage or centre of gravity, sometimes operating from a later stage in optimal circumstances, and at other times reverting to earlier stage perspectives and behaviours when the going gets tough. Our developmental centre of gravity, then, is our default way of thinking and responding to people and the world at this point in our journey.

So, having said all of this, what is the case for undertaking a stage assessment profile?

This is well expressed by Petrie (2015) who suggests they can help people understand:

- Their current stage of development

- The strengths and limitations of this stage of development

- What their next stage of development looks like

- Why people they work with sometimes view the world differently from them

For those who choose to take a stage profile, there are several assessment processes and frameworks available. Whilst it's not my intention to recommend any of these over the others, I will outline some of more established, peer-reviewed offerings. If you decide to take any of the assessments, I recommend you take two or three different vertical assessments, not just one, and ensure that you are debriefed by someone accredited to use the instrument. The optimal approach, especially if you work in a corporate organisation where you can more readily organise a 360-feedback process is:

- A sentence completion assessment such as the Harthill Leadership Development Profile (LDP), Torbert's Global Leadership Profile (GLP), or Cook-Greuter's Leadership Maturity Assessment (LMA).

- A 360 assessment such as The Leadership Circle which provides horizontal feedback on competencies and vertical feedback on psychological and emotional maturity. Or, The Leadership Agility 360 based on Joiner and Joseph's book, Leadership Agility (2007).

- The Subject-Object Interview: developed by Kegan and Lahey requiring a 90- minute face-face interview that is transcribed, scored, and synthesised into a report.

Consolidation

It's important to recognise the purpose of vertical development is not a race to the finishing line. When some people hear about the various developmental stages, and perhaps receive a profile suggesting they're currently at Self-determining/Achiever, the first question in their mind is, how quickly can I can get to Strategist, or better still Alchemist? Their achiever worldview naturally converts vertical development into another achievement exercise.

Though this may seem less exciting, consolidation and integration at one's present stage is just as important as progression. Irrespective of stage, there will always be aspects of a person's experience that they have not fully assimilated and integrated. We don't move forward from one stage to the next with all of our issues closed and fully resolved. The implications of this for vertical development generally, and vertical coaching specifically, is that we must pay sufficient attention to consolidation and not get overly fixated on progression.

Chapter 6.
Executive coaching from a vertical lens

An introduction to vertical coaching

If you're already familiar with coaching you might be wondering what's different about executive coaching from a vertical lens. In essence, this is coaching that's tailored to the vertical stage of development of the individual client. So, whilst working on live content, current issues and problems, these challenges are simultaneously used as learning opportunities to think differently, and come at life differently. The coach seeks to understand their client's perspective taking, expand their worldview and support deeper personal transformation whilst also nurturing curiosity, openness and a desire to grow and develop. The parallel focus on content and the client's evolving way of being is the double-task of vertical development coaching.

A key objective of vertical coaching is to help people deepen their awareness, notice and see more, and be in a position to take a perspective on what was formerly outside of consciousness. In practice, this includes helping the person uncover and understand their deeper core beliefs, assumptions, and worldview because these are the lenses through which they meet and make sense of the world. Bringing these into awareness enables the person to examine and re-evaluate aspects of their meaning-making system – that which creates their 'reality'- and differentiate themselves from it. This enables the person to look at himself or herself, recognize the value and the limitations of their worldview and make judgments about what still holds true and what they may now see as redundant. In other words, to take a perspective on one's own perspective taking, which in itself represents a new capacity.

A familiar example to experienced coaches, is the individual who believes they always have to be the one to take charge, organise everything, and come up with the answers. They may never have seen this in themselves – it's still outside awareness in Subject. Or, it may have been brought to their attention through feedback, yet when moments of truth arrive in daily life, their default is to take over and problem-solve. Whilst there will be positive aspects to this, it may leave others feeling dis-empowered, and frustrated. If the coach is able to work with the individual on this, they are likely to hear something like this – 'I get it but this won't be easy for me to change. Ever since I was small in my family, I was the one to sort things out. I felt I had to

– others weren't really doing what was needed. So, I filled the gap. It's now grown a life of its own and I guess my sense of myself is wrapped up in it. I fix things, that's who I am'.

It's important that developmental coaching includes a focus on lines of development as well as stage development. Irrespective of the centre of gravity a person is primarily operating from, he or she will have grown and developed some lines to a greater extent than others. They may be aware of this but if not, it's likely to emerge from a verbal 360-feedback process. An experienced coach will also notice well-developed and less developed lines of development within the coaching relationship itself, for example, emotional maturity or the lack of.

In line with other approaches to coaching, a core objective is to facilitate shifts, breakthroughs and developmental movement and provide support and encouragement during inevitable fall-backs and periods of regression.

Table 6.1.
The focus of executive coaching from a vertical development perspective

1. Focusing on inner driving forces for growth and development.

2. Helping people understand their current developmental stage and consolidating.

3. Coaching the journey from socialised to self-authored to self-transforming.

4. Helping people become more rounded and balanced by coaching their less developed lines (of development).

The purpose of vertical development coaching

Heightened awareness and expanded consciousness

Awareness is the cornerstone of the developmental process - a key focus and outcome of all personal growth work. Heightened awareness increases self-understanding and the capacity to tune into others. It expands what you can see, what you choose to act on (and how), or choose not to. What was once invisible becomes visible. We've all experienced this. Whilst we may say – 'people don't really change,' it only takes a moment to recognise this is simply not the case. Think about yourself twenty years ago, then ten, then five, then one. You might even see significant changes in yourself in the last few months or weeks. If you've had a recent transformative experience, the timescale could be down to days.

Given the centrality of awareness, it's essential to work with a coach who demonstrates a deeper level of self-awareness and a core competence in how to facilitate heightened awareness and consciousness-raising in their coaching clients.

Sensemaking and perspective

Whilst being able to see more, and see differently, is an important part of the story, letting in other people's perspectives, and potentially being changed by them is equally important. This is one of the ways your lenses and filters change, and when that happens, the world literally starts to look like a different place. New understandings emerge and your meaning and sensemaking becomes more complex and sophisticated. And it really takes on a new dimension when you can step outside yourself in the moment and take a perspective on your own perspective taking and speak from that place.

Greater spaciousness in yourself and for others

This often shows up as a greater openness, more generosity of heart and an expanded ability to 'hold' other people and situations when the situation requires it - and be able to do this without it draining your energy or resulting in resentment.

New capacities

Important new capacities develop during the journey of vertical growth and development. Depending on your current developmental stage, these include:

- Paying better attention in the present moment – noticing more, becoming more receptive and open

- Becoming more reflective and self-aware

- Becoming more relationally skilled

- Listening to learn and understand rather than listening to fix or improve things

- Asking more and better questions

- Becoming more attuned and empathic

- Learning to be in dialogue

- Influencing more effectively

- Appreciating multiple realities and a deeper understanding of resistance to change

- Learning better ways to manage and resolve conflict

- Developing a systems perspective, aware of the inter-connectivity between things

- Expanding bandwidth for dealing with complexity

- Developing the critical executive leadership capacity to think strategically and create vision

- Developing the critical executive leadership capacity to lead larger-scale transformational change

A clearer life vision and a stronger connection with purpose

At different developmental stages, people's sense of purpose can change. As a consequence, new questions arise, which may not go away until you find resolution. Finding the people and right times for these conversations can be a challenge for many people and a key reason why life purpose so often shows up in coaching conversations.

Development across all lines of development

It's relatively unusual to find even-roundedness across all lines of personal growth and development – physical, cognitive, emotional, behavioural, moral, ego and spiritual. The way our lives unfold, and the requirements our family and work roles place on us, preference some lines over others. As a consequence, we become well developed in some spheres, and less developed in others. Understanding the consequences of this can help people understand the results of their 360 feedback processes in a more profound way and point the coaching agenda in the best and most fruitful direction.

A lighter rucksack

Everyone carries one: the question is more about the size and the weight of it. We all have our 'stuff' and personal work. Freedom from being captured by your fears, your unfinished business and your shadow side can be life-changing. Vertical development coaching, depending on the skill-sets and background of the coach, can provide the holding space to open the rucksack and lighten the load

An evolving personal identity and a growing wisdom and maturity

Typically, as we grow, we begin to let go of the need to protect an image of ourselves and our tendencies to over-control, try to fix everything or be right all the time. We pay better attention to others, get interested in helping them grow and live their own unfolding purpose. If you're looking for some overarching phrases that best capture this work, you could call it the journey towards authenticity, wisdom and maturity, or alternatively, the journey of emotional, psychological and spiritual growth. It's the inner journey – the one that Richard Rohr (2012) reminds us, is a 'well-kept secret,' one that 'too few people are aware of or tell us about it'. This journey, the inner journey, is the agenda of vertical development coaching.

Stage-specific coaching issues

Given that the defining feature of vertical coaching is that it's tailored to the vertical stage of the client, it follows that the coach needs to be aware of stage-specific coaching issues. This helps the coach to better tune into the client's overall worldview and work with where the client is right now, as well as where he or she wants to be in the future.

Each adult development stage has its own challenges and what the client wants and expects from coaching, changes at different points in the journey. For example, it's common for people at the skill-centric/expert stage to initially question the value of coaching especially if they understand coaching to be a non-directive talking space. They are likely to equate 'real' help with new knowledge, tools, techniques, and expertise. If they can't see how this can come through coaching, it may not make sense to them, especially when they could be spending their time on horizontal learning where they have a clearer understanding of the promise and the takeaways. This is a reason why some coaches say that people with the skill-centric worldview can be some of the most difficult people to coach. On the other hand, if the coach is able to break through the initial scepticism and introduce vertical growth in a compelling way, the client can find themselves captured by a completely new world of possibilities – akin to entering a room they've never been in before. Some coaches recognise the value of adopting more of a mentor role and intentionally offer their own experience and perspective. This approach may better approximate to the expectations of the client, and if the coach is perceived as credible, then a good rapport can be established.

A similarly good fit can emerge from the Achiever coach working with Achiever clients who are looking for tools, techniques and advice that can contribute to self-improvement, impact results and support career progression. Coaching outcomes and takeaways are often high on the client's agenda because outcomes are what matters most at this developmental stage. However, if the coaching fails to deliver these quickly enough, the Achiever client may soon start their search for the next coach. If the coach is able to add value to the achievement agenda and satisfy enough of those needs, then the possibility can exist for a qualitatively different kind of conversation to emerge.

The following tables give a flavour of stage-specific coaching issues. For a more detailed account, see one of the other short books in the Expand the Possible series - 'Vertical Development Coaching: A Practitioners Guide'. Bluckert 2019.

Table 6.2.
Some examples of stage-specific coaching issues at the conventional stages of development

Vertical stage	Coaching Issues
Conventional stage Group-centric/ Diplomat Socialised	Separating and individuating. Finding your 'authentic' self that is separate and distinct from the group, family and culture. Learning to say no, especially when you feel a strong sense of duty, responsibility and gratitude towards those people. Recognising your own needs, finding your voice, expressing more of your thoughts and feelings, and valuing your own ideas and contribution. Becoming more independent of thought and action. Loosening your attachment to needing to be liked, accepted and acceptable. Daring to be visible, to stand out as different, giving bad news, and facing into the fear of rejection. Learning how to cope with conflict, and better still, how to more skillfully manage it as opposed to avoid it, placate or give in. Loosening your attachment to needing to make things right for others. Disappointment is survivable and inevitable. Note: People with this frame of reference often want a level of clarity about what's expected of them that can frustrate their managers and colleagues who want them to get more comfortable with ambiguity. They also find it difficult to criticize or confront people, and to give bad news, all of which have important implications if they're in management or leadership roles.

Table 6.2. Cont.

Vertical stage	Coaching Issues
Conventional stage Skill-centric/Expert Socialised	Understanding the value of vertical development in contrast to traditional horizontal learning. The coaching agenda is often around self-awareness, becoming more reflective, open, emotionally intelligent and relationally skilled. This usually includes listening better, paying more attention to others, asking more questions and balancing inquiry with advocacy. Committing to understand other people's perspectives and reactions and working with them. The developmental journey is often around 'inner knowing', recognising emotions and developing the capacity to empathetically tune into others. Listening to learn and understand rather than solve things, and experimenting with holding 'correctness' and 'rightness' more lightly. This changes the way you are with people, and consequently, how others are with you. Seeing the bigger picture beyond the detail is often a challenge at this stage and a source of tension with Achiever and post- conventional bosses who can get frustrated. Loosening your attachment to always needing to know, explain and fix everything. Understanding the concept of adaptive change can represent a significant cognitive leap and can open the door to development. Committing to seek out feedback and receiving it in a less defensive manner is important at this stage (and all others). Note: People with highly prized expertise often build a powerful reputation on the back of this, bringing value both to the individual and their organisation. However, this can also be an obstacle to new learning, development and change. After all, why change an identity that works so well?

Table 6.2. Cont.

Vertical stage	Coaching Issues
Conventional Self-determining/ Achiever Socialised	Valuing how far you have already come. Learning to bank your achievements, rather than move on quickly to the next thing, is a common coaching issue at this stage.
	360-feedback often reveals issues around overdone strengths and the relentless drive for results can lead to stress in others and dissonance within teams.
	Deepening self-awareness, becoming more reflective and understanding your inner world continue to be developmental challenges.
	Prioritizing is usually a theme. Becoming less over-extended and focusing more on life balance. Being in the present moment. Finding calm and the 'off' switch.
	Understanding and accepting what you really have control over and what you don't. Letting go of over-controlling and perfectionism. Sharing power and responsibility. Empowering and developing others.
	Becoming less self-critical and more compassionate to self.
	Taking more risks where conflict is present recognising that conflict can serve to deepen contact and improve relationships.
	Listening to your inner voice that may be ready to connect you with a different life purpose beyond accomplishment.
	Note: Achievers can give the impression that anything other than pace, action and results doesn't register as valuable in their eyes. In turn, this can limit the range of conversations that become possible.

Table 6.3.
Examples of stage-specific coaching issues at the post-conventional stages of development

Vertical stage	Coaching Issues
Post-conventional Self-authored Self-questioning/ Individualist	Often more restless and self-questioning around values, purpose and beliefs. This can feel like a stage of not knowing, rich and exciting but also unfamiliar and uncomfortable. Learning to trust the unfolding, often invisible, process can be disconcerting because it won't feel under your control. At the same time, your larger perspective-taking can be exciting even if you're not yet clear what to do with it. Growing into your newly sized container can take some getting used to. Colleagues at the conventional stage can experience Individualists as out of touch with the practical realities of life (on another wavelength, or another planet, as they see it). Despite continuing to achieve and reach goals, if your sense of identity is less invested with achievement, rules and cultural norms, this can be disconcerting and threatening to colleagues. These perceptions can produce relationship tensions. In turn, you can feel misunderstood and misrepresented because others don't always 'get' you. The very real positive benefits of this stage often show up in novel, out-of-the box thinking, risk-taking and wanting to make your own mark. But it's also important to stay collaborative, share responsibility, and stay sufficiently on message, otherwise others may experience you as renegade and unaligned. Staying in touch with people through regularly seeking feedback can be especially important to stay anchored. Dealing with the inevitable changes in your life are characteristic of this stage. These can emanate from inner change but may also play out externally in personal relationships and career decisions. People tend to go through some turbulence at this stage that can be disruptive. Letting go of the need for autonomy and independence is a common theme at this stage. Note: There can be a perception that Individualists are ultimately not team players, preferring to do their own thing. Their need for autonomy can leave an impression that they should to be treated as special cases – a sure source of tension with others.

Table 6.3. Cont.

Vertical stage	Coaching Issues
Post-conventional Self-transforming Self-actualising/ Strategist	Can feel like a lonely place at times so finding the people, the places and the conversations you need becomes increasingly important. However, there are less people around at this stage to have those conversations with, and if you feel starved of them, it can negatively impact your energy, excitement and general mood. Understanding, support and recognition from peers who really see and get you become increasingly important at this developmental stage. Given that Strategists tend to see feedback as vital for growth, you are likely to want, and expect, high quality, insightful feedback from your coach. You may also be looking for new perspectives and novel, edgy experiences which facilitate your personal growth and help you clarify your purpose. Traditional horizontal learning may have become less interesting to you especially if you've discovered transformative vertical growth processes. Because Strategists don't just add to the conversation – they often elevate it to another level, they can sometimes lose people. They are often on the receiving end of projection and transference, both positive and negative. Mentoring others and learning to use self as instrument of change is often an interesting proposition to Strategists.

Coaching the journey from socialised to self-authored to self-transforming

Shifts in identity

Each of these stage transitions, from socialised to self-authoring to self-transforming, represent fundamental shifts in consciousness and perspective together with an emergence of new capacities, including being better able to deal with complexity. At each of these transitions there is a dissolving of the old identity, the self we've constructed. The significance of this is that the new one enables rather than restrains what needs to be tackled at the new stage. These identity shifts are genuinely transformative because they literally change who we are, and our sense of ourselves. From 'I am my group and relationships', to 'I am my role, my knowledge and expertise', to 'I am my achievements', to 'I am my purpose and vision' – these are fundamental changes in perspective and worldview.

Yet we shouldn't underestimate the challenge and complexity of these changes. We often have to go through a period of confusion and not-knowing. Attachment to belonging, being accepted, knowing, problem-solving, being the person who fixes things can be a huge barrier to making a full transition to the next stage. Coming to terms with not being able to predict, control, explain and manage everything represents a significant hurdle to moving forward.

Common transitions

Using the Action Logics language and definitions, the most common transitions observable in organisational life are between Expert and Achiever (a high number of managers profiled using stage assessment instruments are in transition between Expert and Achiever); and Achiever to Individualist – this is the journey towards self-authoring and consolidating at this stage.

If you are locked into the technical worldview where every problem and dilemma can be broken down, analysed and fixed in the same way as engineering issues can be resolved, then you may run the risk of wasting a great deal of your energy and time going around and around the same circles. Many of life's more complex and challenging problems are of a different nature and require a very different approach to them – adaptive change. A change in ourselves. That's not to say there aren't times when we do need to alter some of those material circumstances of our life to become freed up again. What we may miss, however, is that these exterior-focused changes don't always transform things. In these circumstances, we need to be looking elsewhere and recognise that the breakthrough we're looking for has to be an interior change.

Self-transforming

More attention is now being placed on the Achiever to Individualist to Strategist stage transitions because we need more leaders at this later stage to match up to the accelerating rate of change and increasing complexity.

The importance of discovering purpose and vision as part of life's unfolding journey has long been recognised. Maslow in his description of the hierarchy of needs had this to say in 1971;

'Self-actualising people are without one single exception, involved in a cause outside their own skins, in something outside themselves. They are devoted, working at something - something which is very precious to them.'

And at the self-transforming stage a key change is around letting go of the strong need for independence and autonomy and instead, listen to the way in which the world is calling you towards something. You could say that at this stage something larger than yourself, bigger than ambition and accomplishment, is self-authoring you. For those who make this stage shift, the new agenda is often about service.

One of the most significant ways this plays out in corporate leadership is described by Anderson (2018):

'The relationship between drive for personal success and drive for organisational success flips. It goes from big drive for personal success and not that much for organisation, to a complete flip on that'.

One of the most common changes in this journey is your sense of purpose. From the tactical orientation of the Expert to the bigger picture orientation of the Achiever to the visionary orientation of the Strategist, to the transformational change agenda of the Alchemist, an evolution of Self takes place. Along the way, the different skills, habits and capacities required at each stage are developed, or not.

Who can do executive coaching from a vertical lens?

The business and executive coaching field has taken off in the last twenty years and there are many individual practitioners and coaching firms offering executive coaching services. In addition, developmentally focused organisations have created their own internal capacity for leadership coaching. Some have supported their internal coaches to develop to an advanced level and a few have taken specialist training in vertical development coaching. So, there are coaches out there who can work in this way but it will be a small minority of the total number of practicing executive coaches. This is in large part because the field of vertical development practice is still in its infancy and there are very few postgraduate level vertical coach training programmes. There is also another factor and it's highly significant to the efficacy of vertical coaching - the coach's own developmental stage.

The coach's own developmental stage

In the coaching relationship, there are two worldviews in play – the coach's and the client's. Many developmental researchers believe that the match between the vertical stage the coach is operating from, and the stage the coachee (client) is operating from, is critical to whether developmental coaching can really take place. A commonly held view is that a coach at the same developmental level will be able to coach effectively as a supportive presence, provide help with problem-solving and work with behavioural agendas. In other words, the coach has the capacity to support their client at the stage they are currently at – always assuming they are there themselves. However, they may fail to notice when their client is showing signs of transitioning to the next stage.

Being understood is a gift: being missed, not so good...

The issues of efficacy and effectiveness come into play if the coach is coaching someone a stage, or more, beyond their own. Here there can be problems of mis-diagnosis, misunderstanding, and misinterpretation.

In a series of articles about vertical coaching, Rybeck (2016) underlines this point with a personal story:

'Seeking support with a career transition, I shared with my coach how I found parenting to be one of the most profoundly significant experiences in my adult life. My coach responded by asking questions about how I might explore work in the child care field given my enthusiasm for child-rearing. This line of inquiry took me aback. Parenting was so much more to me than kid care. How could my coach not have seen that? What did he hear in what I said that provided a view of my experience so different from what was true for me? I felt unseen and misjudged by his response as I had a deep, not fully recognized, desire to contribute to something much bigger than myself that channelled the passion and commitment that came through in my parenting and yet, went far beyond the mechanics of child rearing. The coach, operating from a skill-centric mindset had focused on the skills and tasks needed to succeed as a parent. He was encouraging me, as with strengths-based coaching, to build on what I am good at. Nothing wrong with that – except that it missed what was really going on for me'.

It's likely that anyone reading this who has experienced coaching will have had a similar experience of feeling 'missed' by their coach. You may have also thought – this coach is competent, listens well, asks good questions, can be supportive; but I'm not sure he can help me get to the next level.

Brown (2013) takes the view shared by many in this field:

'It is important when choosing a coach or consultant that not only have they done vertical development work before, but they should hold an action logic that is at least one developmental stage more complex than yours. This enables them to challenge you into deeper and more nuanced perspectives than you typically hold yourself.'

Endnote

If Executive Coaching from a Vertical Lens is of special interest, you will find an extended version of this material, including a detailed methodology, a thorough description of stage-specific coaching issues, examples of coaching questions, and the Gestalt approach, in another publication in this Expand the Possible series entitled: Vertical Development Coaching: A Gestalt-Based Practitioners Guide.

Chapter 7.
Senior team development from a vertical perspective

From a culture change perspective, there's a clear rationale for senior team coaching using a vertical development approach. If you believe that the beliefs and decisions of the senior leadership team "create a vertical ceiling in the organisation that is hard for others to advance beyond," then it follows that "when you elevate the thinking of the ET, you raise the ceiling for everyone else, unleashing a much previously locked-up potential. The most effective way to shift the vertical development of an organisation is to shift the mindset of the Executive Team". Petrie (2014). When this happens, it gets noticed by the senior leadership population and can to lead to a new sense of optimism which energises and frees people up.

This uplift in the worldview of the senior leadership team leads to new perspectives on old problems, better thinking and strategising, which in turn can turn into more productive action. But this is more than mindset change – it's whole-set change. Vertical growth and development is about expanding what people can see and the sense they make of it. But if this is to lead to transformational change it must translate into new capacities and consistently role-modelled mature leadership behaviours. This requires individual members of the team to commit to personal work – in essence their unfolding developmental journey. This includes their thinking but needs to go beyond thinking and into the emotional and ego development aspects of vertical growth. When personal work only focuses on thinking – cognitive development – we run the danger of developing imbalanced, heady people who intellectually understand concepts such as emotional intelligence and empowerment, but are unable to connect with their own and other people's feelings nor let go of the power and control required to enact empowerment.

However, it would be naïve to think that these messages will always be well received by senior leadership teams - on the contrary they're invariably met with a great deal of resistance, at least in the first instance. And this is perfectly understandable. As a group of individual contributors, each member of the senior executive team is likely to be giving the very best they can. They don't know what more they could give. And those with a more developed team ethos will also be working together as best they can, paying good attention to collaboration, support for colleagues and the common team purpose.

For these and other reasons, making a serious commitment to the vertical development of the senior team is a challenging proposition and a journey that most teams have yet to make. That doesn't necessarily mean that they haven't engaged with team interventions at all. Most executive teams have undertaken a range of team processes such as: outdoor team building, team profiling such as Belbin's team roles or MBTI, facilitated team conversations, and business simulation exercises.

Each of these methods has its strengths and potentially adds value to an executive team. Outdoor development takes people out of their familiar environment, providing a cultural island where the normal rules don't apply. Numerous teams have gained rich insights into issues of leadership, team dynamics and group cohesion through engaging in this type of learning experience.

Psychological profiling raises awareness of preferences, styles of relating and can promote the positive aspects of difference. Business simulations stretch teams intellectually and reveal core strengths and weaknesses. Facilitated team conversations provide a space for quality group dialogue around critical business challenges and group process issues.

The common ground is that they heighten awareness, facilitate stronger contact and connection between people, raise energy and foster group engagement and identity. Team members generally come away from them with a better understanding of how their colleagues tick and the relationship dynamics in their team. They also provide an important forum to clarify team purpose, build trust, deal with tensions and conflict and agree what kind of behaviours people want to see in their team.

It would be hard to imagine any serious sports team going into a competitive game without putting the hours in on the training pitch first. The team interventions referred to above are the corporate equivalent of that training pitch. These 'time-outs,' as they're commonly known, are where leadership teams can learn together, celebrate what they're doing well and become more aware of unproductive patterns of behaviour. They can then experiment with new ways of operating together to function at a higher level.

The emergence of team coaching

Historically many of these team interventions were based around the Away-Day model or workshops of two or three days in duration with follow-ups. More recently there's been a growing awareness that longer term, more extensive programmes of team development are required to reliably embed team learning. Whilst occasional team days and short intensive workshops have often had a powerful short-term impact, the persistent challenge has been the transfer of learning and behaviours back into workplace. Teams regularly report that they've taken two steps forward only to make one step back within just a few weeks or months. This is the context from which team coaching has emerged as a compelling team development intervention.

The distinctive approach taken by many team coaches is to focus interventions at three levels of system aimed at:

1. Improving the team as a unit/system

2. Improving the relationships within the team

3. Improving the skills and performance of the individual members of the team

A common feature of team coaching processes is that the team coach, sometimes working with colleagues as part of a coaching team, delivers a series of team workshops whilst also coaching the individual team members in parallel. Facilitated sessions between pairs or small groupings can also feature in this approach.

Team development from a vertical lens

From a vertical perspective, there are two further goals in addition to the three already described: namely, transforming the level of development of the team whilst supporting vertical stage development of the individual members. And if it's the executive leadership team, the additional agenda is the transformation of the organisational culture.

So, we can now put these together and see the full scope of senior team development from a vertical perspective:

Table 7.1
The agenda for senior team development from a vertical perspective

---

1. Improving the team as a unit/system

---

2. Improving the relationships within the team

---

3. Improving the skills and performance of the individual members of the team

---

4. Transforming the level of development of the team whilst supporting vertical stage development of the individual members

---

5. Transforming the organisational culture

The specific skill-sets and capacities that accelerate vertical team development

Key skill-sets

During the team development journey, it will become apparent which of the skill-sets vital for effective team functioning are strongly, or not so strongly, developed. Focused attention will need to be paid to improving these in order to properly equip the team to transform. The most common of these tend to be:

- Emotional intelligence

- Process awareness

- Coaching skills

- The capacity to engage in dialogue

These are all skills that facilitate self-awareness, empathy, deeper listening, better questions, feedback and recognition of others. They also promote deeper self-reflection, emotional self-management and relationship building. Teams who learn these skills together become more conscious of their team dynamics and more equipped to tune into one another's needs with sensitivity and care. These skill-sets provide a team with a much-enhanced resource for dealing with conflict whilst also facilitating a higher level of collaborative behaviours.

Key capacities

A number of key capacities were identified in the previous chapter on individual coaching and these are given additional momentum from the team coaching process. Important new capacities develop during the journey of vertical development. Depending on the current developmental stage of the individual team members, these include:

- Paying better attention in the present moment

- Becoming more reflective and self-aware

- Becoming more relationally skilled

- Listening to learn and understand rather than listening to fix things

- Asking more and better questions

- Becoming more attuned and capable of empathising

- Learning how to be in dialogue

- Influencing more effectively

- Appreciating multiple realities and understanding resistance to change

- Learning more skilled ways to manage conflict

- Developing polarity thinking and a systems perspective

- Expanding bandwidth for dealing with complexity

- Developing the critical executive leadership capacity to strategise and create vision

- Developing the critical executive leadership capacity to lead larger-scale transformational change

Cascading individual and team development throughout the organisation

Whilst this section has focused on executive team development, it will be evident that this approach is relevant and applicable to any team within an organisation, and needs to be cascaded through-out the leadership population if the strategic agenda is about cultural transformation.

Indeed, Anderson (2011) concludes 'that there is no organisational transformation without a preceding transformation in the consciousness of the leadership'. His proposition is based on the idea that there is an inter-dependence between all levels of the system. The organisational system cannot organise at a higher stage of development than the leadership. And until the system organises at the new level of order, it hinders the development of most people in the system. Beyond that Anderson posits that 'only as the bulk of the population (of an organisation or society) develops to the new stage of development is there a possibility for the system to take its next evolutionary leap.'

Group-based learning experiences that develop vertical skills and capacities

The very same skill-sets and capacities described earlier – emotional intelligence, process awareness, coaching skills and the capacity to engage in dialogue need to be more widely developed in many organisations. They are powerful enablers of vertical development and are best learned, or improved, in group-based workshop environments. They then need to be practiced over and over again until they become integrated into the individual's way of seeing and being in the world. When that happens, this provides the most powerful evidence of effective leadership development.

Endnote

If Senior Team Development from a Vertical Perspective is of special interest, you will find an extended version of this material, including a detailed methodology, and the Gestalt approach in: Vertical Development Coaching: A Gestalt-Based Practitioners Guide, another publication in the Expand the Possible series.

Chapter 8.
Deep-dive vertical development leadership programmes

It's still the case that most leadership development programmes are heavily steeped in the horizontal method where delegates are provided input on leadership theory, case studies, competency-based skills frameworks and models of explanation, delivered primarily through lectures, PowerPoint presentations, and small-group discussions. The very language used to describe these programmes reflects their conventional nature – classroom learning, training courses, leadership seminars. Energisers and experiential exercises are often in the mix to break things up, but the overriding approach is outside-in, informational learning, delivered by scholars, and management trainers.

Vertically-oriented leadership programmes are still fewer on the ground despite the fact that there have been versions of these running in many parts of the world for far longer than the vertical development concept has been around. Experiential programmes to raise self-awareness and enhance interpersonal skills in managers were first introduced in the mid 1940's using methods that would still be new and progressive to many people today. The T-group methodology, which Kurt Lewin and associates helped to develop, was an example of the experiential approach in action. The purpose of the workshop experience was to increase awareness of self and others through facilitated group dialogue and feedback. Valuing and appreciating difference was at the heart of the method. That original work lives on today through the NTL Institute who have trained literally tens of thousands of people in their core methodology.

Some of the earliest applications of Gestalt within management and leadership programmes are attributed to Richard Wallen and Edwin Nevis. Beginning in 1959, they used awareness-raising techniques within sensitivity training groups for managers and this work can be seen as a forerunner of today's emotional intelligence programmes.

Contemporary versions of these experiential programmes have kept this tradition alive and pushed at some of the same frontiers encountered by the original pioneers. The best of these provide opportunities for what Joiner and Joseph call, reflective action which is the process of alternating between immersion in the experience and stepping back to reflect and learn from it.

The benefits of vertical leadership programmes

Vertical development programmes:

- Can act as triggers for vertical development because they tend to be uplift experiences where people make significant breakthroughs and shifts in themselves. For some people, it can be their first experience of deeper self-exploration in a group context.

- Provide the skilled help, experiential conditions of safety, non-judgement, high trust and high support necessary for transformative growth.

- Foster a tight, supportive group experience, where deep relational connections are forged, some of which continue long into the future.

- Can be an important reflective space where someone first 'sees' what they have been formerly Subject to, such as core beliefs, social conditioning, and big assumptions.

- Can be a safe enough place (sometimes the first place), where there is sufficient support and trust to share one's truth at a deeper level, break the pattern of holding in, open up, and feel the feelings.

- Create the conditions for deeper self-disclosure and safe experimentation

Programmes of this kind are usually experienced as intensive, powerful and memorable events. It's not unusual for people to refer to them as life-changing, and say that they've come back to themselves. They've re-connected.

The Courage and Spark© vertical development programme

One such programme, Courage and Spark©, designed and delivered by the author and colleagues within a number of global organisations, is an example of this. An immersive, five-day residential workshop, Courage and Spark© uses a Gestalt approach to accelerate vertical development in both senior leaders, and next-generation, high-potentials.

The objectives of the programme align with the broader goals of holistic vertical growth and development and includes processes that:

- Heighten awareness at three levels: self-awareness, 'other' awareness, and process awareness

- Deepen contact and connection

- Focus on healthy self-regulation

- Facilitate closure around issues and unfinished business

- Facilitate the integration of previously disowned parts of oneself

- Enable new perspectives to emerge

- Reveal big assumptions

- Provide feedback on impact

When this programme has been rolled out to the senior leadership population in large organisations the personal development benefits listed above have been augmented by significant change at the system level. The experience of deeper self-disclosure with a colleague group has transformed relationships and beyond that, the leadership culture.

Chapter 9.
Case vignette

I close with a case vignette that brings together a number of the themes of this short book. It's a real story and it begins some years ago when I was invited by the CEO and Group HR Director of a medium-sized retail company to engage with them on an ambitious organisation development programme aimed at shifting the cultural centre of gravity, beginning with the executive leadership team. An externally-led cultural audit had diagnosed this company as a 'red organisation'. This had disturbed the CEO and other organisational leaders, though in truth, they accepted it as an accurate assessment. It became their burning platform for action.

They committed time and resources to changing the situation and they started by taking a long, hard look at themselves as the companies' most senior leadership team. They could see that their previous ways of addressing these issues had mostly been technical – one thing after another had been tried, usually after a good deal of fighting between them as to the relative merits of the so-called solution. The strangest thing about all of this was they had all worked to some extent and yet, the bigger challenge remained relatively untouched. They began to understand that they could go on finding and implementing technical solutions forever, or at least until they were so old and fed up that they would hand the reins over, but the real challenge they were facing would never be solved that way. It required adaptive change – change in themselves and especially around relinquishing power and control.

This was a significant insight and represented a shift of perspective - one that many leadership teams in organisations and political life never get to. Recognising it in the first place and making the interior changes in themselves were, of course, two entirely different things.

So, using a reputable stage assessment profile, they discovered that one out of their seven members profiled at Red (Opportunist), five at Orange (Achiever) with one operating from Green (Individualist). What they also noticed, as did the next tier of leaders, was that under pressure, many of them had a tendency to fall-back to red behaviours. And they were often under pressure. This made life together as an executive team very hard and exhausting: it also made for a tough and stressful life for their direct reports.

What followed was an intensive period of vertically-oriented interventions led by myself and my team which included: individual and senior team coaching; team coaching cascaded throughout the company; large-group workshops to bring everyone into dialogue; our Courage and Spark© vertical leadership development programme; and a highly structured coaching culture programme across the entire company.

The results were slower to arrive than the executive leadership would have liked. They were mature people but, as with most leaders, impatient to see progress in each other and themselves - a perspective shared by the vast majority of senior managers.

This, however, is a good news story. By their own assessment, and confirmed by re-running the original organisational culture audit, there was a significant shift in the organisation culture with a new centre of gravity at Orange and some pockets of Green. The journey of development of the executive leadership team played an important part in the bigger transformation story. Progress was uneven and hard-won – joy and disappointment went hand in hand over a timescale of four years. When they again profiled individually using the same stage assessment instrument, one member was assessed at Teal (Strategist), two at Green (Individualist), three at Orange (Achiever) and one at Amber (Diplomat). This shift at the top was visible to the rest of the company and was met with a mixture of surprise and delight.

The CEO's own personal journey was a revelation to him reflected in these comments:

- I'm conscious of how I am now. I can see the impact I have on other people – before I couldn't.

- It's helped me find my purpose. I will continue to be the CEO of this company but there is something far more important now and it's this – I want to devote my life to developing my consciousness and helping others do the same.

- I'm sharing my journey with others, not just my leadership team, but also the other managers, and they're sharing them back. They never did that before.

- These new conversations are about how we want to work and live – what our purpose is together. They are developmental conversations, not about task or results. It's the best part of my day.

- I really do think we've matured both psychologically and emotionally.

Further reading and resources

Anderson (2011). The Spirit of leadership. The Leadership Circle.

Benner, D. (2012). Spirituality and the awakening self. Brazos Press.

Bluckert, P. (2019). Expand the Possible: The Gestalt Approach to Vertical growth and Development. TBP

Bluckert, P. (2019). A Comprehensive Guide to Vertical growth and Development.

Cook-Greuter, S.R. (2004). Making the case for a developmental perspective. Industrial and commercial training, 36(7), pp.275-281.

Cook-Greuter, S. (2013). Nine levels of increasing embrace in ego development: A full-spectrum theory of vertical growth and meaning making.

Cowan, C. and Beck, D. (1996). Spiral Dynamics: Mastering Values. Leadership and Change. Blackwell Publishers.

Gallwey, T. (2000). The Inner Game of Work. Random House.

Garvey-Berger, J. (2012). Changing on the job. Stanford Business Books.

Kegan, R. (1994). In over our heads: the mental demands of modern life. Harvard University Press.

Kegan, R. and Lahey, L. (2009). Immunity to change. Harvard Business Review Press, Boston, MA.

Kegan, R. and Lahey, L.L. (2016). An everyone culture: Becoming a deliberately developmental organization. Harvard Business Review Press.

Joiner, W.B. and Josephs, S.A. (2007). Leadership agility: Five levels of mastery for anticipating and initiating change. John Wiley & Sons.

Laloux, F. (2014). Reinventing Organisations. Nelson Parker.

Petrie, N. (2013). Vertical Leadership Development – Part 1 Developing Leaders for a Complex World. Center for Creative Leadership.

Petrie, N. (2015). Vertical Leadership Development – Part 2 Developing Leaders for a Complex World. Center for Creative Leadership.

Revans, R. W. 1982. The origin and growth of action learning. Brickley, UK: Chartwell-Bratt.

Rooke, D. and Torbert, W.R. (2005). Seven transformations of leadership. Harvard Business Review, 83(4), pp.66-76.

Rooke, D. (1997). Organisational transformation requires the presence of leaders who are strategists and magicians. Organisations and people, 4(3), pp.16-23.

Rybeck, J. (2016). Coaching vertically. Copia coaching and consulting.

Torbert, W.R., & Associates (2004). Action inquiry: The secret of timely and transforming leadership. Berrett-Koehler Publishers.

Watkins, A. & Wilbur, K. (2015). Wicked and Wise. Urbane Publications.

About the author

The founder of Courage and Spark©, practice leaders in the vertical development field, Peter Bluckert has created and led four international organisation development consultancies. During a consultancy and coaching career spanning nearly forty years, working with executives and teams from a wide range of private and public-sector organisations, Peter has built a reputation as both a thought-leader and innovative designer of transformational learning experiences. His desire to see improved standards in the field of Executive Coaching led him to join forces with other coaching pioneers and co-found the European Mentoring and Coaching Council (EMCC) in 2000 and he remains committed to this work.

Best described as a Practitioner, rather than Academic, he believes that good theory strengthens good practice and has published two coaching books (Psychological Dimensions of Executive Coaching and Right Here Right Now: Gestalt Coaching) and several journal articles. He is currently completing a new book on the Gestalt approach to vertical growth and development.

Peter is regularly asked to speak at International Conferences and has delivered presentations and programmes in Europe, the US, Asia, The Pacific and Africa.

Please feel free to get in touch.

grow@peterbluckert.com • www.peterbluckert.com

About Courage and Spark©

I want to briefly introduce you to Courage and Spark©. Firstly, why the choice and combination of words here? You probably already have a feel for it. The nature of 'inner-work', deeper self-exploration, is of itself a courageous act. Many people avoid it if they can, and only do it if their lives get too hot to handle. Spark? Because when people really re-connect to themselves, almost like coming back home to themselves; when they get unstuck; and when they get in touch with their purpose and vision, there is a release of energy. You can often see the moment when the spark occurs. Re-ignition. A re-awakening and a renewed appetite for life.

Since establishing the company in 2010 my team and I have been privileged to deliver our vertical leadership programme to managers and leaders in a wide range of companies and on three continents. There have been a lot of sparks with a lot of courageous people and we've been delighted by the way it's been received.

In addition to our Courage and Spark© signature vertical leadership development programme, we offer a wider range of learning experiences to help people grow vertically. These include:

- A one-day route-mapping workshop to explain vertical development, and act as guide to how the journey can unfold.

- Vertical development coaching – both at the individual and team levels.

- Practitioner development for coaches and consultants in the Gestalt Approach to Vertical Growth and Development.

- A Knowledge Centre about the 'how' of vertical growth and development – including our books, white papers, articles and podcasts.

Please feel free to get in touch.

grow@courageandspark.com • www.courageandspark.com

Also in the 'Expand the Possible' series:

If this short book has grabbed your interest and you want to take it forward you may wish to know that this is part of a series of 'Expand the Possible' books covering vertical growth and development. Other books in the series include:

- **A comprehensive guide to vertical development**

- **Vertical development in the workplace**

- **Vertical development coaching: A Gestalt-Based Practitioner's Guide**

- **Vertical development: How it happens and how to accelerate it**

You may also be interested in two previously published books by Peter Bluckert: